CREATIVE EDUCATION

WASHINGTON REDSKINS

JULIE NELSON

Published by Creative Education
123 South Broad Street, Mankato, Minnesota 56001
Creative Education is an imprint of The Creative Company

Designed by Rita Marshall

Photos by: Allsport USA, AP/Wide World Photos, Bettmann/CORBIS,
SportsChrome

Library of Congress Cataloging-in-Publication Data

Nelson, Julie.
Washington Redskins / by Julie Nelson.
p. cm. — (NFL today)
Summary: Traces the history of the team from its beginnings through 1999.
ISBN 1-58341-063-5

1. Washington Redskins (Football team)—History—Juvenile literature.
[1. Washington Redskins (Football team)—History. 2. Football—History.]
I. Title. II. Series: NFL today (Mankato, Minn.)

GV956.W3N45   2000
796.332'64'09753—dc21   99-015751

First edition

9 8 7 6 5 4 3 2 1

Washington, D.C., is the only major city in America not located in one of the 50 states. The city, named after the country's first president, George Washington, has been the United States' national capitol since 1800. It is located in the District of Columbia (D.C.) on the Potomac River between the states of Maryland and Virginia.

Washington is home to such famous structures as the Capitol, the White House, the Washington Monument, the Lincoln Memorial, and the Jefferson Memorial. Washington is also the home of a professional football team known as the Redskins. In 1937, George Preston Marshall moved the

Sammy Baugh (#33) led the Redskins to greatness.

team from Boston to Washington. The Redskins had entered the National Football League in 1932, but they never won the support of Boston's sports fans. Attendance was poor even when the team won the NFL Eastern Division title with a 7–5 record in 1936.

The following year, when the team moved to Washington, Marshall put his Redskins players in gold pants and brilliant burgundy jerseys—uniforms guaranteed to catch the eye and make a statement. Marshall also decided to make the game more entertaining for fans and gave them pro football's first big marching band. The band, along with fireworks, circus acts, and wild animals, became part of Marshall's halftime entertainment. In its first season in Washington, the team would be just as impressive.

1 9 3 7

Rookie Sammy Baugh began his Hall of Fame career, passing for 1,127 yards.

SLINGIN' SAMMY LEADS THE 'SKINS

Before the Redskins moved to Washington, Marshall signed outstanding collegiate quarterback Sammy Baugh to a contract for the 1937 season. Baugh's powerful, accurate arm was a rarity in the 1930s. The young quarterback had displayed his remarkable ability during his college days at Texas Christian University. "Even from the first, we were amazed at many things in Sam," said sportswriter Amos Melton. "He had great confidence in himself even as a freshman. He was never flustered on the field, whether he was winning or losing."

When Baugh got to Washington, some sportswriters and fans wondered if the man they called "Slingin' Sammy" was tough enough for the demanding world of the NFL. "Take

High-powered halfback Stephen Davis.

my advice," the famous sportswriter Grantland Rice told Marshall. "If you sign him, you'd better insure his right arm for a million dollars, because the tough guys in this league are going to tear it right off of him."

In training camp, Baugh didn't take long to prove to the Redskins coaches that he was not only tough, but confident as well. One day, head coach Ray Flaherty was drawing a pass play on the blackboard. He drew an X, then said to Baugh, "When he [the receiver] gets here, Sam, I want you to hit him in the eye with the pass." Baugh replied, "Sure, Coach. Which eye?"

With Baugh and running back Cliff Battles leading the team, Washington clawed to the top of the Eastern Division in 1937, pummeling the favored New York Giants by a 49–14 score in the final regular-season game to clinch the title. The Redskins ended their first season in Washington with a berth in the NFL championship game.

A week later, the Redskins traveled to Chicago to face the powerful Bears. No one expected the Redskins to win, and their prospects looked especially dim after Baugh dragged himself to the locker room at halftime with Washington behind 14–7. As a trainer looked over Baugh's sore and battered knee, Baugh said to him, "Tape me together. I gotta get back into the game."

"They're gunning for you, Sam," the trainer said. "You could get seriously hurt out there." Baugh, only two quarters away from a championship, was not about to quit. "Nobody's gonna knock out Sammy Baugh today," he replied. "The team needs me. Can't win without passin', and I'm the Redskins' passer."

1 9 3 7

Fan support built to a fever pitch as the Redskins stormed to an NFL championship

Baugh returned and destroyed the Bears, passing for 335 yards and three touchdowns by the game's end. Receiver Wayne Millner caught two long touchdown passes, and the Redskins won their first NFL championship, 28–21. Marshall came up to Baugh in the locker room after the game. "Not bad for a beginner," he said with a smile.

Baugh's passing led the Redskins to another Eastern Division title in 1940. Pitted against the Chicago Bears again, the Redskins would fall short this time. George Halas, Chicago's legendary coach, revealed a new pattern known as the T-formation: three running backs in a single line behind the quarterback. Early in the game, it became clear that the Redskins did not know how to counter the T.

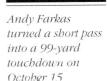

Andy Farkas turned a short pass into a 99-yard touchdown on October 15

The Bears ran up the score, scoring one touchdown after another. By the end of the game, the score was 73–0. Marshall was stunned. His Redskins were dazed. "We had the greatest crowd in Washington's history, and we played our poorest game," Marshall lamented.

The Redskins quickly rebounded after their embarrassing loss, winning the Eastern Division in 1942, 1943, and 1945. Washington defeated the Chicago Bears 14–6 in the 1942 NFL title game but lost 41–21 to the Bears in 1943 and 15–14 to the Cleveland Rams in the 1945 championship game.

Slingin' Sammy became one of Washington's most well-known citizens. Supreme Court Chief Justice Fred Vinson discovered one day just how famous Baugh was when a youngster asked Vinson for two autographs. "Why do you want two?" Vinson asked the child. "Are you getting one for a friend?" "No," the youngster answered. "I can swap two of yours for one of Sammy Baugh."

Record-setting quarterback Joe Theismann.

Swift cornerback Darrell Green.

1 9 5 0

The Redskins became the first pro team to have games televised.

Baugh played his last season in 1947. As the Redskins prepared for Baugh's final game in Washington, teammate Joe Tereshinski climbed on a bench and yelled to his teammates, "There he goes—the greatest. He's the best football player we'll ever see. Let's make certain he doesn't get any mud on his pants today." Baugh went out in fine style, firing six touchdown passes to trounce the Chicago Cardinals 45–21. Washington fans would have to wait almost 25 years to root for another playoff team.

A SONNY OUTLOOK FOR WASHINGTON

In 1964, Marshall traded away veteran quarterback Norm Snead and brought in Christian Adolph Jurgensen, known to most as "Sonny." Short, compact, and strong-armed, Sonny Jurgensen reminded Redskins fans of Sammy Baugh. Jurgensen had a powerful arm and overwhelming confidence, two things the struggling Redskins needed badly.

Joe Theismann, a quarterback who joined the Redskins in the mid-1970s, marveled at Jurgensen's strong arm and bullet spiral passes. "Boy, could Sonny throw," Theismann said. "If you wanted a tight spiral down the field that would land absolutely perfect, Sonny was your man."

Despite Jurgensen's power passes and the talents of wide receivers Bobby Mitchell and Charley Taylor, the Redskins' win-loss record wasn't impressive. Except for a 7–7 season in 1966, Washington posted losing seasons every year from 1956 to 1968.

Hoping that a coaching change would make a difference, Marshall hired Vince Lombardi in 1969. Lombardi, who had led the Green Bay Packers to five NFL championships and two Super Bowl titles, had retired from coaching after the 1967 season. Marshall was persuasive, though, and Lombardi agreed to take the reins of the Redskins.

As the season opener approached, Lombardi reminded his new team that he had never coached a losing club. "And nothing is going to change that," he warned. Inspired by Coach Lombardi's confidence, the Redskins finally broke their losing streak, finishing with a 7–5–2 record in 1969.

Sonny Jurgensen best voiced the team's new attitude. "Just working under this man is the greatest opportunity I've ever had," he said. "I told Mr. Lombardi that in five days, I learned more from him than in my 12 years as a pro." Unfortunately, the 1969 season would be the only chance Jurgensen and his teammates would have to learn from the master. Before the 1970 season began, Lombardi was struck with cancer. Two months later, he died. Later that year, George Marshall died as well.

As the football world mourned the loss of the two legends, new team owner Edward Bennett Williams brought in George Allen as coach. Allen had built the Los Angeles Rams into winners, and he vowed to do the same with the Redskins. He immediately began trading future draft choices for veteran players. Fans began calling the Redskins the "Over the Hill Gang." Allen made several deals with his former team, the Rams, for linebacker Jack Pardee, defensive lineman Diron Talbert, and safety Richie Petitbon, all of whom were more than 30 years old.

Allen's gamble paid off. The "Over the Hill Gang" made the playoffs in 1971, finishing with a 9–4–1 record—the

1 9 6 5

In a comeback win over Dallas, Sonny Jurgensen threw for 411 yards.

team's best since 1945. The 1972 Redskins, led by quarter-back Billy Kilmer and running back Larry Brown, soared to the top of the NFC Eastern Division. In the NFC championship game, they defeated their longtime rivals, the Dallas Cowboys, 26–3. The Redskins' run was finally stopped in the Super Bowl by the undefeated Miami Dolphins, who pulled out a 14–7 win.

1 9 6 8

Bobby Mitchell ended his Redskins career after gaining a team-record 8,162 yards.

THE THEISMANN THREAT

In three of the next four years, the Redskins made it to the playoffs but never to the Super Bowl. After a 9–5 season in 1977, George Allen was fired and replaced by Jack Pardee, the former Redskins linebacker. Allen's experiment with the "Over the Hill Gang" had kept young talents such as Joe Theismann on the bench, and Pardee intended to change that. "You can help build the future of Redskins football," Pardee told Theismann. "You've paid your dues. Now it's time to take charge and get this team rolling again. The future is now."

For Theismann, the promotion to starting quarterback was the realization of a dream. "Some people want to be doctors or lawyers or presidents," Theismann said. "I wanted to be a quarterback. All my life, I looked for the secret to making that dream come true."

Unlike the pass-oriented Jurgensen and Kilmer, Theismann relied on both his arm and his legs to beat opposing teams. Theismann could be spectacular, but he could also be erratic. To help Theismann correct his mistakes, Pardee brought in Joe Walton as the Redskins' offensive coordinator

Joe Theismann's favorite target, Art Monk.

The star of Super Bowl XVII, fullback John Riggins.

in 1978. Walton took the young quarterback under his wing, showing him ways to improve his game. "Walton took the time to make me a better football player," Theismann recalled. "He taught me how to think in a game, how to analyze my technique, how to move."

The Redskins found immediate success with Theismann and Pardee, running up a 10–6 record in 1979. Running back John Riggins led the ground attack, while rookie wide receiver Art Monk gave Theismann a reliable target. The Redskins' defensive bulwark was massive 300-pound lineman Dave Butz. Pardee earned NFL Coach of the Year honors, but his luck soon took a turn for the worse. In 1980, the Redskins fell to 6–10, and Pardee resigned as head coach. "I love the Redskins too much to watch them lose," he explained.

1 9 7 6

Linebacker Chris Hanburger led a smothering Redskins defense.

Williams filled the coaching vacancy with former San Diego Chargers head coach Joe Gibbs, who returned Washington to the Super Bowl in only his second season. Theismann and Riggins keyed an offense that rolled up 83 points in three NFC playoff victories. This offensive performance was balanced by a peerless defense led by ferocious ends Dexter Manley and Charles Mann. As in 1973, the Redskins would face the Miami Dolphins in the Super Bowl.

Theismann was thrilled to finally become a part of Super Bowl history. "As a kid in New Jersey," Theismann reflected, "I wanted someday to be in Joe Namath's shoes or Johnny Unitas's or Bart Starr's. Now, here I stand. Pinch me, I want to see if this is real."

By the third quarter, trailing 17–13, Washington knew that it was real—and that the title was within reach. Theismann, desperate to spark his team, attempted to float a screen pass

Like Theismann, Mark Rypien was a great leader (pages 18-19).   17

John Riggins carried the ball 375 times and scored a team-record 24 touchdowns.

over Miami's Kim Bokamper. The linebacker jumped high in the air and deflected the ball straight up. But Theismann didn't panic. Throwing himself forward, he knocked the ball away as it fell toward Bokamper's hands, breaking up an almost certain interception.

In the final quarter, Riggins scored on a 43-yard run on fourth down, helping him set a Super Bowl record with 166 rushing yards on 38 carries. Behind Riggins's running, the Redskins pulled out a 27–17 victory to bring the NFL championship back to Washington for the first time in 40 years.

The Redskins' winning ways continued in 1983, when Washington compiled a 14–2 regular-season record and then earned playoff victories over the Los Angeles Rams and the San Francisco 49ers. The Los Angeles Raiders, however, ended Washington's winning streak 38–9 in the Super Bowl.

Theismann spent two more seasons with Washington before a badly broken leg ended his playing career. Jay Schroeder replaced him at quarterback until he too was hurt in 1987. Young and untested Mark Rypien was available for quarterback duties, but the Redskins turned instead to Doug Williams to take them back to the top.

Williams was a veteran who had shown great talent—and equally great inconsistency—during his long career. He had quarterbacked for Tampa Bay during the late 1970s and early 1980s before playing three years with the United States Football League's Oklahoma Outlaws. When the USFL folded, Williams found himself in a backup role in Washington. "There were no starting quarterback jobs available in the NFL," Williams explained. "The Redskins were the only team that called me. What else was I going to do?"

In 1987, Williams worked magic for the Redskins. In the playoffs, Washington rolled over Chicago and Minnesota to make it to its fourth Super Bowl. However, few people except the Redskins players and coaches believed that Williams had the potential to be a reliable leader in the big game. Williams realized that he had a golden opportunity to prove himself to his critics. "It was destined," he said. "It was in the cards."

Williams and the Redskins apparently saw something in the cards that few other observers would have predicted: victory. Washington racked up five touchdowns in the second quarter and went on to trounce Denver 42–10. Doug Williams had a record day, throwing for 340 yards and four touchdown passes.

Defensive end Charles Mann tore into opposing backfields, making 14.5 quarterback sacks.

Lineman Joe Jacoby gave Williams great pass protection.

Confident quarterback Doug Williams.

Williams injured his back in 1988 and spent much of the season on the bench. The team's only reserve quarterback, Mark Rypien, was called on to fill the gap. Although the Redskins' defense was torn up with injuries and the team posted a weak 7–9 record in 1988, Rypien turned in a strong season. Coach Gibbs then had a difficult choice to make: which quarterback to choose as the starter the following year.

Rypien won the starting job but began the 1989 season with a puzzling losing streak. With Washington at 5–6 late in the season, Rypien finally broke out of his slump, passing for 406 yards to beat the Bears 38–14. The Redskins never looked back, finishing with five straight wins and just barely missing the playoffs. Rypien ended the season with a Pro Bowl appearance.

The Redskins began their seventh decade by posting a 10–6 record in 1990 and returning to the playoffs. An opening-round win against the Eagles was followed by a 28–10 loss to San Francisco, ending the Redskins' hopes for a Super Bowl shot.

But the next season, Coach Gibbs's 11th year with the team, the Redskins returned to the Super Bowl and demolished the Buffalo Bills 37–24. Super Bowl MVP Mark Rypien completed 18 passes and threw two touchdowns. Many of his throws ended up in the hands of Gary Clark and Art Monk, who each caught seven passes. Cornerback Brad Edwards added two interceptions, and the Redskins' defensive line sacked Buffalo quarterback Jim Kelly five times.

1 9 8 9

Joe Gibbs became the seventh-fastest head coach in NFL history to reach 100 victories.

Fleet-footed wide receiver Gary Clark snagged 70 passes for 1,340 yards.

Joe Gibbs spent one more season directing the Redskins before retiring in 1993. He left after leading Washington to a 140–65 record, eight playoff appearances, and three Super Bowl berths in 12 seasons.

Finding someone to fill Gibbs's shoes was a tall order. The team's first choice was longtime assistant coach Richie Petitbon, who led the Redskins to a feeble 4–12 record in 1993. Norv Turner, who had been the Dallas Cowboys' offensive coordinator, then stepped in. Turner promptly committed himself to rebuilding the team, cutting many former standouts when limits were put on professional salaries. Although Washington stumbled to a 3–13 season in 1994 and a 6-10 record in 1995, Washington fans and management saw signs that the franchise was headed in the right direction.

Relentless running back Earnest Byner.

One of the brightest signs came in the form of free agent running back Terry Allen. In five seasons with the Minnesota Vikings, Allen had made NFL history, becoming the only runner to have reconstructive knee surgery on both legs and then come back to rush for 1,000 yards. The hard-charging back signed with Washington in 1995 and posted back-to-back 1,000-yard seasons. His 1,353 yards in 1996 set a new franchise mark, and his 21 touchdowns led the entire league.

Halfback Terry Allen led Washington's ground game with 10 touchdowns

Behind Allen's heroics, the Redskins won seven straight games in 1996 and finished the season an improved 9–7, narrowly missing the playoffs. Quarterback Gus Frerotte established himself as the team's new starter, taking every snap for Washington.

1997 marked the debut of Washington's FedEx Field, the largest outdoor arena in the NFL. The Redskins christened the 80,116-seat stadium with a thrilling overtime victory on September 14. In the overtime period, Frerotte connected with receiver Michael Westbrook for the 40-yard game-winning score to upend the Arizona Cardinals 19–13. Although the Redskins once again just missed the playoffs in 1997, their 8–7–1 mark gave them a second straight winning season, something no other NFC East team had achieved in the two-year stretch.

Still, Redskins management made big changes in 1998. In an effort to strengthen the team's run defense, Washington signed two 315-pound defensive tackles: Dana Stubblefield, the 1997 NFL Defensive Player of the Year, and Dan "Big Daddy" Wilkinson, the first overall pick in the 1994 draft.

Swift wideout Michael Westbrook (pages 26-27).

Linebacker Ken Harvey led the defense for a fifth and final season.

Despite the additions, Washington's defense ranked among the NFL's worst in 1998. The offense also sputtered as the punchless Redskins lost their first seven games of the year, including a 41–7 thrashing at the hands of Minnesota—a disastrous start for a team that many experts had predicted to win the NFC East. "People get caught up in talent—talent isn't the issue," a frustrated Coach Turner said. "It's being efficient, executing, and obviously we aren't playing consistently. That's the issue." Although Washington reeled off four consecutive wins late in the year to end the season 6–10, Redskins fans clamored for more changes.

Washington released Terry Allen, the franchise's third all-time leading rusher, along with quarterbacks Trent Green and Gus Frerotte before the 1999 season. Redskins manage-

Powerful pass rusher Dana Stubblefield.

ment then looked west and found their new quarterback: Brad Johnson.

Johnson was widely considered to be the best non-starting quarterback in the NFL in 1998. At the beginning of the season, the longtime backup had been poised to guide the Minnesota Vikings' powerful offense before injuries landed him in a backup role yet again behind All-Pro Randall Cunningham. The 30-year-old Johnson, wanting to be a starter, asked to be traded after the season.

Washington pounced on the opportunity, trading three draft picks for Johnson. Redskins general manager Charley Casserly was confident that he finally had the player that would make the difference. "I think we have made it very clear to everyone that we are going to improve our football team this season," he said. "Brad Johnson is a highly regarded quarterback and has proven that he can take a team to the playoffs."

Washington continued to bolster its roster in the 1999 NFL draft by taking Champ Bailey with its first-round pick. Bailey, who had left Georgia after his junior season, could play either cornerback or wide receiver and was an equally dangerous threat on both sides of the ball. "From the minute he stepped onto the field, it was obvious he was the best athlete out there," recalled Greg Williams, an assistant coach at Georgia. "He would do things during practice that made you shake your head."

Johnson proved to be a valuable pickup, triggering a suddenly-potent Redskins offense and marching the team to a 10–6 record and the AFC East title. Playing injury-free for the first time in several seasons, Johnson aired the ball out

1 9 9 9

Albert Connell racked up 1,132 receiving yards to help spark the Redskins' offense.

29

One of the NFL's most accurate passers, Brad Johnson.

Defensive back Champ Bailey.   31

for more than 4,000 yards. He also fired 24 touchdown strikes, most of them to the talented receiving duo of Michael Westbrook and Albert Connell.

The Redskins hosted the Detroit Lions in the first round of the playoffs. Although the Lions had thumped Washington 33–17 earlier in the season, the Redskins took their revenge with a 27–13 win. Running back Stephen Davis, who had topped the NFL in rushing touchdowns during the season, led the Redskins with 119 rushing yards and two touchdowns.

Washington's season ended the next week in Tampa Bay, however. After jumping ahead 13–0, the Redskins fell 14–13. Washington had a chance to steal the victory in the closing moments, but a bobbled field goal snap put the game out of reach. "It was a tough game to lose," said Michael Westbrook. "We didn't finish them off when we had a chance."

After adding linebacker LaVar Arrington, quarterback Jeff George, and defensive end Bruce Smith in the off-season, today's Redskins have the talent to compete with the best teams in the league. In fact, it may not be long before the nation's capital is again home to an NFL champion.

2 0 0 1

Fans expected young linebacker LaVar Arrington to become a dominant force.